Subtracting with Seals

By Charles Sellers

Gareth Stevens
Publishing

Please visit our website, www.garethstevens.com. For a free color catalog of all our high-quality books, call toll free 1-800-542-2595 or fax 1-877-542-2596.

Library of Congress Cataloging-in-Publication Data

Sellers, Charles, 1979-
Subtracting with seals / Charles Sellers.
    p. cm. — (Animal math)
Includes index.
ISBN 978-1-4339-5672-0 (pbk.)
ISBN 978-1-4339-5673-7 (6-pack)
ISBN 978-1-4339-5670-6 (lib. bdg.)
1. Subtraction—Juvenile literature. 2. Seals (Animals)—Juvenile literature. I. Title.
QA115.S45 2011
513.2'12—dc22

2010051703

First Edition

Published in 2012 by
Gareth Stevens Publishing
111 East 14th Street, Suite 349
New York, NY 10003

Designer: Haley W. Harasymiw
Editor: Therese M. Shea

Photo credits: Cover, pp. 1, 5, 7, 9, 11, 13, 15, 17, 19, 21 Shutterstock.com.

Printed in the United States of America

CPSIA compliance information: Batch #CS11GS: For further information contact Gareth Stevens, New York, New York at 1-800-542-2595.

Contents

Boldface words appear in the glossary.

Two Homes

Seals live in water and on land. They live where there are a lot of fish.

3 seals – 1 seal = 2 seals

Seals have four **flippers**. Flippers help them swim fast. They help seals get around on land, too.

3 seals – 2 seals = 1 seal

Seals find their food in the water. They love to eat fish. They eat other small sea animals, too.

4 seals – 3 seals = 1 seal

9

Seals close up their noses when they are underwater. They must come up for air, though.

2 seals – 1 seal = 1 seal

11

Bulls, Cows, and Pups

Boy seals are called bulls. Girl seals are called cows. Baby seals are called pups or calves.

4 seals − 2 seals = 2 seals

Eared Seals

There are three groups of seals. Eared seals have **flaps** over their ears. They walk using all four flippers. Sea lions are one kind of eared seal.

5 sea lions

− 2 sea lions

3 sea lions

Earless Seals

Earless seals have no ear flaps. They **wriggle** like worms across land. Harbor seals are one kind of earless seal.

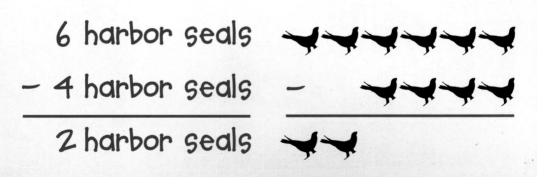

6 harbor seals

− 4 harbor seals

2 harbor seals

The elephant seal is an earless seal. It is the largest seal. Some are more than 16 feet (4.9 m) long!

5 elephant seals
− 4 elephant seals
─────────────────
1 elephant seal

Walruses

Walruses are seals, too. They have long **tusks**. They use their tusks to climb onto ice. They also fight with their tusks.

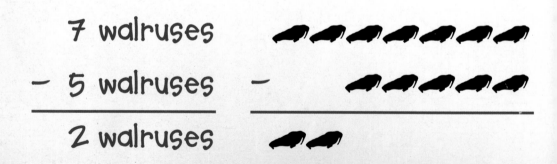

7 walruses

− 5 walruses

2 walruses

Glossary

flap: a thin piece of skin that covers an opening

flipper: an animal's wide, flat body part that is used for swimming

tusk: a large, pointed front tooth that sticks out of the mouth

wriggle: to move by twisting and turning the body

For More Information

Books

Fuller, Jill. *Toy Box Subtraction*. New York, NY: Children's Press, 2004.

Sexton, Colleen. *Seals*. Minneapolis, MN: Bellwether Media, 2007.

Websites

Harp Seals

kids.nationalgeographic.com/kids/animals/ creaturefeature/harp-seals/

Learn about an earless seal called the harp seal.

Subtraction Fun!

www.fun4thebrain.com/subtraction.html

Play math games that help you practice subtracting.

Index